CHRISTIANITY IS BACK

Some poems after modernity

Alan Storkey

Christian Studies Press,
Cambridge

Alan Storkey

(other books A Christian Social Perspective, Transforming Economics, The Epistemological Foundations of Consumption Theory, Marriage and its Modern Crisis, The Meanings of Love, Jesus and Politics, War or Peace – the long failure of western arms, Militarism has failed – We disarm the World)

© Christianity is Back
First edition 2024

Christian Studies Press,The Old School, High Street, Coton, Cambridge CB23 7PL

alan@storkey.com

We live in God's Creation and it's big.
We see the glory and it is our home.
God feeds us richly, usually when we dig,
And we are stewards, growing from the womb.
Our thinking, mainly, is Your after thought
And we learn good within your great commands.
We under stand and see what you have taught,
and, wise or fools, your gentle love still stands,
but lost and sinners we mess up the place.
We even spoil the planet you have made.
We've worshipped us, the selfish human race.
And manufacture slavery in our trade.
We do it wrong. We even egotize.
Now we repent, and grow more Jesus wise.

CHRISTIANITY IS BACK.

It will perhaps soon become clear that Christianity is back. Modernism, the faith that we are marching successfully into the future is disintegrating. We are going towards global warming, to patterns of personal disintegration, to fighting one another, the threat of human annihilation and to hundreds of millions of suffering people. We urgently need respect for God's creation, the tools of self-criticism (sin) and the way back to the good human Christian truths we can walk in.

This collection of poems is cobbled together, but it does some of this journey. It begins with a longer, slightly sweeping big story poem, setting out some of the case, then moves to Post-Modern Easter examining the same written thirty-five years back. This obviously owes to T.S. Eliot who long before had seen the problems of modernism.

The collection then works through the themed Christian story of Creation, Sin and Jesus Christ. The Creation sonnets, usually unrhymed, reflect the glory of God's creation as revealed in science and normal life, structuring the way we live and who we are in a post-evolutionary world. The normal secular scientific awed voice to cover the now believable exquisite creation gives way to acknowledging our Creator with gratitude. Maybe the consequences of human beings knowing they are created are not developed enough in this section.

Then we look at human sin. The churches tend to focus on individual sins, and ignore the rich biblical understanding of national, cultural, imperial, social and economic sins, and these sonnets may help widen this, especially in relation to militarism.

Then there are some Christian and salvific themes flowing out as deep good news for our days and nights.

Perhaps humanity is moving towards some kind of crisis, not just tragic for some, but really for us all, and we need the wisdom and self-examination of the Christian faith to address the human condition direct in 2024. We are back in our long, often tragic, human history and are not so far from the problems of Babylon, Jerusalem and Rome, but now things are moving fast.

Forgive its weaknesses. It is just a signpost. I hope it helps. Some of the sonnets are linked to paintings. So happy, and unhappy, dipping, reading, thinking to put alongside your own wonderful poetry of life. My thanks to Mum, Dad, Elaine and many, many more…

Alan Storkey, Coton, 2024

Contents.

And Jesus said, "When you pray..." Our Father, Who art in heaven. Hallowed be thy Name. Thy Kingdom Come. Thy will be done. Give us this day. And forgive us our trespasses. As we forgive those. And lead us not... But deliver us from evil. For thine in the Kingdom. The Prodigal Son. Jesus in Cambridge. Coton Church. God's Scargill Community. Confetti Day. The Red Admiral. And did those feet. And so, dear Pilate. The Dove of Peace. Imagination. Underground. We stand for Peace.

The Failures of Western Modernism.

We won the War, again, but really lost,
because we, too, were evil when we won.
We Bomber Harrised Germans in revenge
and did the dams, a triumph for our side.
The Second War destroyed the world once more.
Progress was regress, but the West had won,
and we were right, and even right again,
against the suffering heroes of the East,
the evil Commies who had won the war,
then scapegoats as MacCarthy hunted them.
The empire people now were losing it,
and the US would rule its "equal" world.
Truman, the small, had bombed Hiroshima
and make the Pentagon our new born king.

We gathered for the peace at the UN,
but Churchill pulled the Iron Curtain shut,
We painted evil Soviets as Red,
and Long March China soon became our foe.
The Brits, in debt, quit India, and knew
their Greatest Empire was a shrinking plot.
The Land of the Free, (after slavery)
would rule the world, its culture and its way.
It armed for peace, and soon had many arms;
the octopus of peace fought army wars.
It fought for right in Cuba and Vietnam.
It Nietzsched Freedom under Washington
and then imposed on all Democracy.

We won the War but lost another one,
To know the truth and meaning of our lives.
The human race now quickened to a sprint.
Our truth is best, we knew in the New World,

The modern birthplace of the ego self,
Self-reference was our usual library,
We lost our sin and the young ruled all pop,
Expressing truth in every which way loud.
My truth, of self-made progress, had the stage,
bought and now sold with credit on the nod.
And we, like sheep, have turn-ed our own way,
And human failure is now off the screen,
We are the moderns, Elvis confidence,
The self-congratulation West has won.

We had all learned – Democracy had come.
All people mattered (in our little patch).
We knew the world must grow a different way.
Aristocrats were hiding in big homes,
while Council Housing, Health and Pension Plans
made life for normal people sound again,
and companies were for the public good
not profit for the few monopolists.
We even thought a fair wage for the poor,
and governments are servants of us all,
and it was good for many, as the scars
of total war were healed in passing years.
Yes, it was good, but only good in parts,
For soon another problem hove in sight.

We lived in the economy of Keynes.
Production and consumption went around.
So nations grew; the workers worked quite hard,
and income was, for now, distributed.
We manufactured, making things for us,
Growth was success, and more was better than
The life we had before with fewer things.
More, ever more, in money was our goal,
And money grew to wealth in little piles.
This money was the met wand of our lives.
We worshipped Mammon and it was in charge,

and oil would oil our fast flung, shallow lives,
and empires grew to multinationals,
and they knew best and hid the coming costs.

The baby boomers were now spoiled and right.
The young could do themselves and dump
The long-life learning - two millenium,
They all did pop, and self-expression banged
On a drum accompanied by guitar,
Ourselves, uncritical, will rule the world.
Our wants will fuel mass consumption stores,
And make advertisements our life-time guides.
We then found credit, mortgaging the years
ahead with wants and instant privilege,
and let the banks make money, untold wealth,
Until the pluto-rich emerged again,
and Mammon ruled the Thatcher-Reagan years,
to run the world on open throttled greed.

Along the way were many little gods,
Which kept modernity enthroned to grow.
We must go fast, and then fast back again.
We owe it to ourselves, when we do not.
We worship different personalities,
and politics becomes consumer choice.
The truth becomes the slogan, not half true.
Technologies are plastered over wrongs,
and power as control is back in power.
"I did it my way" was the funeral hymn,
when my way messed our next gen families up,
and we were all made passive by TV,
watching the lives of others as our own,
our lives unliving in remote control.

Our thinking looked for simple certainties.
Of reason, objectivity or choice.

We followed science, or the theory of
whatever discipline we lived within
at university, but not in life.
Knowledge was power, if it was funded well,
but really thought was slowly fading out,
as media learning came to dominate
and business studies soon was in control
while economics lost the power to live.
Our thinking was what could compete the best
within the realm of loudest media noise.
The truth was hidden, far too poor to last,
in proper gander empires on full blast.

We lost much of the written past to now,
Few read Isaiah, Moses, John and Paul,
Or even Tolstoy, Eliots and Donne.
We started with old Hemingway, and then
The new-born literature arrived,
all struggling with the now, as Realists,
or even to escape from where we are.
But then the word lost out to the TV
and tens of hours of viewing in a week.
It all zoomed past in manufactured sight,
and living in the word, the long word life,
was lost, the instant screening of the soul.
The Word-made-flesh, the test to word the truth,
was off our screens, we followed flickering.

The self was growing, first the girl and boy
saw through the silly power of the man.
Elvis was fun but not the way of life,
And girl power, sexed, was coming round the bend.
The ego-centred self environment
was made a mess by all that we now need.
The psyche hidden personality
Was plastered on our screens and in our lives.

Our politics became a person choice
Which buried principles beneath the face.
We wanted to be like, an image thing,
No longer God, but him on the TV.
The self exploded, with conflicting parts
From every orifice, loud sounding farts.

Meanwhile world history was moving on.
We stock piled nuclear weapons everywhere,
Costing the earth, although they were not used.
Then suddenly the Soviets had gone,
And Russia filled with western oligarchs,
The ideology of wealth had come,
And making money governed everyone.
The West extracted all it needed most
From round the world to keep its people rich,
and multinational companies cost the earth.
They ran the world and most elections were
sorted to keep them in big yachts off shore.
They had control and flat denied the truth
of their big greedy quickly heating world.

We lived and loved, but not as God would have,
Us poor in spirit, big in charity,
But feeling love and broken marriages,
Our fragile egos scattered far and wide.
Building new lives was left to the mass media
And adults rationed children by the hour.
"I want" was not a good way to relate,
And more, not less, was difficult for most,
And self-congratulation was half false,
And luxury was still a well-worn chair.
These lives, projected out of advert dreams,
were good or bad in terms of really love.
While we claim selfish failure as success,

we reap the truth of love as sheep and goats.

The West has blustered, looting round the world,
And fighting, if needs be, or We need War,
It rules the UN, thinking it is right,
But it is much like Rome and slavery,
It messes up through power, East and West,
But God will bring the mighty from their thrones.
We will fall down; the others are awake,
They see the gods that we are worshipping.
And do not see the deep humility
The truth required to be good neighbours to
The world God also loves, those just like us.
And so we come now to Jerusalem,
and God says, Your self-righteousness you dump
and beg forgiveness. Jesus Christ is Lord.

POST-MODERN EASTER

*(written over several Easters around the events of
the Iraq-Kuwait-Allied forces war, jury service at
Harrow Crown Court and the Spring Harvest Easter
Celebration at Butlin's, Minehead)*

Is this the death wish?
We go to war with the bloody whore,
spend a hundred billion, and destroy far more,
kill a hundred thousand, mainly theirs, dead,
and widows cry alone in bed.
Houses are flat, power stations still,
a stunning victory, full of goodwill,
guns for oil and oil for a gun.
Why did Jesus suffer and harm no-one?

Is this the death wish?
the life untenable on other terms
than curtain down? setting its face
into the sunset, flaming heroics?
No media mediator, the last reel,
road end with nails in wood,
but detailed care for friends, mother,
enemies, deliberate death
by murderers identified and faced
calm.

We are not lost, being in the wrong place.
Our location is correct with respect to the rest
of creation, but we are lost
on Oxford Street or in Trafalgar Square.
Where will the West End, young man?
Oh, taxi, take me to the Square;
I want a pigeon sitting in my hair,
and all directions take me everywhere.

Please do not tell me I'm already there.

Unlike Presidents,
God does not need to think big, being
equally at home with large and small.
Thunder and palaces are a bit infra-dig
when you have made the whole show anyway.
What you say carries weight, hey, gravity,
just because you are God, whether
anybody listens or not. Why
would people not listen to God?
They must have something on their minds,
or want him to shout, or think big,
or work to a different agenda.
Are you whispering, God,
or should we turn the radio down
and cup, cup, cup our ears.

London commuters go to work
and rock with roll of train,
develop skills, enjoy a perk,
drop eyes and home again.

Homes eat the bodies; TVs start;
advertisements sell food,
which end as a domestic fart,
humanity subdued.

So busy people fill their homes,
with shopping, DIY.
The washing up bowl gently foams;
they grow alone and die.

The black cloud hangs over the land and
is called victory. Those who do
not know defeat, own goal cheers. Here's
the firework sound of nation celebration

while deathblood flows, foe's woes.
Important people manufacture praise; PA's glaze.
The stratosphere of lies, flies, defies
the gravity of the situation.
World leaders grave pave
the road to hell with good intent, bent.
The black cloud hangs heavy over the land and
God cries with heavy rain, pain.
Defeat for humankind, signed unkind
Us, again, again.

Now know a holy fear before your God,
the great Provider, good and wholly true,
the purest crystal, leaf and droplet Lord,
who makes with care the lepidoptera,
creation's loving user friendliness.
The darkness dwells within, spills oil,
so cynic, dirty, how our oil is black,
and we must shudder at our really lives,
and only good is good enough.
Excuses all wear out before their time.
Or we will frighten God
and shoo him off. We'll make
the everything afraid of us. Boo
Christ, you must be scared of us.

How dare this man be so familiar
God. No "I'm the greatest" stuff, or "look
there's nothing scares me in the universe."
but "See the Father here before your eyes.
You silly people, don't you see that God
is here with you right now. I love you all.
You are my children, friends and intimate.
I live within your hearts, the Whisperer.
You wear my uniform; I am your boss
and pay you always more than you deserve.
Sit in my lap and know identity;

you have my genes and I know who you are.
You rest together tender in my care.

So inevitable the middle-class pride, drive
upwards to quiet, made-it glory on my own terms,
the shell, and slow realisation of not working,
patching up, making the best of a bad job life.
Or nice beneath the superficial flaws.
Why have they left the room?
Or lock my heart in a deposit box
safe from assault and beating, dead.
Or live dynamic, switching on the sleep
at half-past one with pills,
to kill the making sense,
background alive.

We are at risk if people talk
direct to God. Love, joy and peace destroy
our powers. We need criss-crossing fear to drive
their lives. With kids enjoying God
and all this easy access to the Almighty,
things could get out of control.
We've got to kill him soon
or our whole system crashes to the ground.

Late train, again, and later night.
Great Western Railway almost out of sight.
The West is set in post-modernity,
mock Georgian concrete for eternity.

So creeps the East to West,
Deflating the great pride.
The middle way is best;
the great white hope has died.

Success has suffered much
and true and false are dumb.

De-solve yourself and melt.
The vacant stare has come.

So blind, we cannot see
creation is so good;
we live now through TV,
the pearl misunderstood.

The fingers of God's hand
caress the East and West,
touch cultures in each land.
The humble poor are blessed.

How can you hate wise innocence
and seek to murder him,
to plan him dead? Dry rot strands
grow into furry calculations.
Trapped, we decay,
too late to go back,
escalatored down.

It is not here; it is not there;
you cannot find it anywhere.
But stay and wait and see
how full God's rule in you can be.

Hug, wrap around, enfold your lonely man
and keep the bitter cold out if you can.
He'll come inside you looking for the womb,
but fearing lest he find your home a tomb.
Love is so complex; private parts so tight;
the who is in there always out of sight.

"What will you ride, Sir? How will I order?"
"That young ass, and bring its mother too,
lest it be frightened by the crowds."
No warhorse, feet scarcely off the ground.

They're right, but so, so deeply wrong.

You sightsee through the world with souvenirs,
buy the can here and can't remember where
you saw it on the screen sometime before
and give it now a hundredth at f8.
The distance of the world resides within,
the smoked glass screening of the soul.

It is really difficult to conceive how any
sane man, man mark you, could screw up
so fully as to betray him for funds, Him,
healer, coughing up pearls and gentle too,
spreading love, like muck on barren land.
What was in Judas' mind? Bloody money.
Sometimes I think we are all going down
the tubes.

"So, Judas, leave now, go and take the purse.
Your friends believe you're going to buy bread.
You've had this opportunity to face your curse,
but now you've calculated, go ahead
without recriminations, nothing will be said."

And so we come to trial. Harrow Crown Court.
All good and true, but one perhaps. She knits
oblivious, deciding on the facts,
no post-Tractatus judge, but Tory sleep
of rentier law and order rich.
The lady wears her blindfold.
O Lord, have mercy on us.
The victim is guilty, yes, but knitted up
by the big mother, tape worm on lap.
Where are the big house, greedy rich
for whom we work, whiter than white,
the milking class, porn, city, shares,

drugs and monopoly, big dealing class?
Our Pharisees? They've moved
to get the nasty taste out of their mouths.
The automatic milkers are at work.
And so we come to trial.

No time for truth - nearly two thousand years.
The current problem is the populace,
their clamour fed by morsels, carefully dropped.
Keeping things ordered is a daily race.

Ten thousand problems, carefully seen through,
all by one man, here, looking at your face.
He sees the structure of your Godless Rome
and why the Empire will not last the pace.

The people are a problem for him too.
They want a sign, a miracle in case
their neighbour love runs out and turns to hate.
No votes for him; truth always in disgrace.

The opium is the TV and the press.
The Sun shines down its arse and makes a mess.
So Murdoch makes the monarchy his tool
and drugs and tarts the nation, dies rich fool.

Why, God, did you not listen to our arguments
for your existence, rationalize yourself,
speak when you are spoken about,
and take up residence in our academic heads.
They were quite open-minded, logical.
You could have been an avant-garde Idea,
established by our books and articles.
You lacked ambition of our intellect.
A simple-minded God can't go down well.

No accident, that war, nor yet the next.

The US pushed out BP,
installed its puppet Shah and milked the oil
from mogul empires in tall offices.
Then Jimmy Carter's naive principles
of human rights upset the applecart.
The Ayatollah severed hands and cut
the arms trade, but we financed war,
sold weapons, built up debt, Saddam Hussein,
Iran-Iraq, tame weapons and the Gulf,
used smoking Bush to service limousines,
and pardon North, the White sepulchral House.
So silly Saddam does not know the rules:
buy weapons; do not use them; play your games.
A wicked victim, hollow President.

How do you understand conspiracy?
To kill the Son of God, a grand design,
the evil one, or two, or all of us?
the increments of sin, small private thoughts,
clever, not holy, not considered wrong,
just selling pigeons at a premuim
to fodder people, selfish calculus.
The picture is a pixel pattern lie,
conspiring with, against, defeating us.

Here is the Word redeeming all
the flabby self-indulgence of our words,
the formal maps and tailored cadences,
the pneumatic authority of arguments,
elaborate categories, dilettante shaped,
destructured in the foolishness of God.

You cannot make the journey, nor can I,
but come along the track a little way.
Say you were good, and gave and gave and gave,
fed, healed and cared for crowds who followed,
but, when it counted, chose a murderer.

Say you withstood all evil when it grew,
and carefully exposed its origins,
until the predators all turned on you,
saliva venom, hating all you did.
Say you as teacher shared the greatest thoughts
with those you'd nurtured through to understand.
They, vacuous, threw the pearls away.
Does not self-pity work within your soul,
resentment that this good should be so spurned,
and anger than such truth is trampled on?
The more you know and love, the lonelier,
the deeper good, the greater gulf between.
And then to know they want to crucify
God's love expressed in you.
Now love them more, nasty and fickle,
blind after wickedness and fools,
yearn for their lostness, care less
for death, know and forgive.
Then lose yourself, the Father in your heart,
and freely sacrifice your very self,
for this dear scum.

Each tortured day of horrorscopes will leave
this question hanging on your consciousness.
This man was killed by such
as walk our streets,
sick unto death.

You, naked on the cross.
We know our shame
and look away.

This quiet morning, stretch, tender my side.
Your sunshine, Father, warms yellow on blue.
Nothing to do. Death over. Now you guide
these little ones to us and all is true.

How does the Spirit rest upon our time?
Not uninvited, but not absent now.
No future fast or living blick by blick,
but when we hear, no ashes or regret,
nostalgia, polishing the past.
God's time has come, is now and now.
Each heartbeat hits the moment,
just, true and good.

Where, Lord, this Easter will you visit us,
Cathedrals, mountain tops or Holy Land?
Please come to Butlins, welcome with us here
in Crazy Horse, Big Top and Beachcomber.
You may not like pink mermaids, plastic trees
and fake stone walls. Your style is Spring and wind-
swept hail. But slum and harvest hearts. We give
an alto sax, voice, arms and tear-stained face
to praise you, resurrected Lord. Not death
but Ishmael's stomp. Not vain, proud, grave, all
lost,
but clappy happy mad and bouncing praise.
So easy God with us, for us; beneath
our weakness, failure, mercy-swinging grace.
Dear Jesus, friend of sinners, all-in Lord.

So, is it merely a happy ending?
God wins on Easter Day,
defeating death and bastards everywhere,
the cosmic V sign to the human race?

Thus we confront our superficial selves,
that cannot live one life, stay in one skin.
We even posture with the truth. Our words
still try to gloss our evil and injustices
like Nixon's tapes. But stop.
Now God is with us, everything exposed,

knows us and suffers all in sovereign love.
All things are changed, but really as they are.
We dwell now in the passive mode
and watch the ego silver fish run from
the light of Christ transforming all the world,
dead sinful selves, no death wish,
life.

1990-4

Creation Sonnets.

NO SIGNATURE.
God, without paintbrush, come and paint the year,
Big canvas, never framed, and always here.
You take your time, build slowly, sort light dark,
Prepare the ground, earth wet, keep contrasts
stark.
Start with dark twigs, drip wet with diamond snow
Or prick dot milky way on indigo.
Perhaps you need red tulip, hearted black
Before white wedding hedgerow, blue eggs crack.
Keep colours hidden fresh in little seeds.
Like Dürer, make a masterpiece of weeds.
My mother's lily and my father's rose,
like summer bombs, cool, livid love expose.
Time ochres, kharkis, russets grass and trees.
We view the final glory on our knees.

BIG UNIVERSE.
So cold, beneath the wide star studded black
This God created universe, this one,
With Catherine milky wheel diagonal,
Here in its edge, one little galaxy,
All smudges in this vast immensity,
Expanding from the first great divine "Yes",
When everything was sorted as is now,
We live and look at twinkles in the sky.
This is not ours. We have a little share,
No rent, but clouds and rain and moon rich sleep.
To you-ward only can our lives make sense,
To come and go like charmed particles,
Good as you warm our souls to look beyond
And know ourselves eternal stayed in you.

APPLAUSE. (*Snape*)
Conductor bows acknowledging applause,
Sweat pouring down his nose and in his eyes.
His is the music and the different scores.
He even crafted all the instruments
And got the orchestra together over time –
His time, when you go far enough before.
His sound as well, he made the air vibrate,
His are your ears and brain and memory.
He made the members of the orchestra
And pre-designed construction of the hall.
You know this concert grafted in your bones.
The tunes each morning, evening and night
Soar through your life, and have no movement
pause.
Before it ends, now, clap and roar your praise.

BEHIND SNAPE MALTINGS.
Cathedral sky vaults over flat salt marsh,
not dark, but eye-hurt grey, rebuilt each hour.
Endless shard reeds change places, back again,
light headed totter from the coming shower.
Breathe wind, and stir the grasses' frequencies
in holy exhalation of pure praise.
Hiss hymns, slide dunlin, quiver drops off leaves;
make distant river water glitter craze.
Stand, swallow, undecided on your tail.
Peel off, you screaming swifts and slash the glare.
Flap out, sad heron, beaten by the wind.
Wheel, seagulls, and find liquid in the air.
Behind: Snape Maltings. Wild applause before,
performers clapping, always God's encore.

I CAN'T BELIEVE
So, you believe no God created this,
no great design, but just a happenstance,
not personal, but rather hit or miss,

not even aim, but just a primal dance
of stupid chemicals. Yet even they
need pre-constructing into atom, quark,
from which non-aiming hits, you say,
the universe was made. Shots in the dark,
no guns, no big N "Nature" doing things,
sand with IQ (but not computer chips)
has done it all. The cosmic order springs
from elementary particles with slips.
I can't believe - unless the quarks have phones
and don't pay extra for more distant zones.

SEEING CLEARLY
To see with holy sight each gift of God
can happen only when my ego's gone.
A shallow self is grafted to my eye;
I see the world through mirrors which reflect
Back vanity, out angled stereotypes,
A hall of mirrors, pride distorting all.
The shaving image holds me in its grasp.
No smashing free, but to be seen through God,
Creature of millions, yet with numbered hairs,
No outward view, but loved with visage marred.
So, darkened, face each detail of the world
crafted by God, not other than it is,
and gasp in awe creation is so good,
so blind my normal use of human sight.

FAST AND SLOW.
So, slowly I paint rocks for several days,
Building the texture, modulating greys,
Until Achmelvich's sheep strewn crag appears
Clothed with stiff grasses, wind bent bouncing ears.
But you have started several billion years
Before my flat, pathetic, instant fix.

There is the era before molecules,
Space sprung gigantic galaxies evolve,
Slow without form and void through to the earth.
Then, even slower, rocks as treacle bake
With crystals set in granite, lost to sight,
And buried to mature three billion years.
So shrinks our human quick fix arty stuff
Before the glory of your slow, worked craft.

GOOD MORNING, GRANTCHESTER.
Hello, says God, Good Morning, Grantchester.
Today we have a rose and yellow dawn.
No need to hurry. Toast and coffee time.
It took me something like a billion years
To slow the Cam, long sedimentary work,
That none of you have seen, beneath the grass.
So start the day with joy and breathe in deep.
Make this day good, whatever work you do.
Keep selfishness at bay and look around
At all this glory, meadow, willow green.
Remember I like children more than you
And greet your Coton neighbours with a nod.
Accept this day from me. Let it proceed
In mill-pond peace and kindness to the eve.

PRIVET TIME.
The moment of each day awaits its time.
Today, the small leaved privet hedge,
Ignored again by every passer-by,
Is clothed in frost, minutely round each leaf.
Not overdone, white on a tailored coat;
The leaves themselves, cold darkened, have repose.
But now in grandeur small they hold their place
In God's creation on this frosty morn.
But that is not enough. Now gone we know
Not where, the spiders, have abstracted out

Their great expressions, on the canvas hedge,
Amazing space, in diamonds, no flies,
with frost. I notice, as I walk, and stop,
the non-anthropic glory of God's world.

MAPPING THE CREATION
Start, God, the awesome process with your word.
Think out dimensions and embody time
without a ready, steady, total tick.
All must begin, bang, ready to unfold,
a cosmic order bigger than our brains,
built structures studied in the biggest labs,
vast energy encrafted to a shape,
acceleration of the elements.
The raging fire explodes ex nihilo
And all we are begins to orchestrate
Creation. Science charts some of Your work
In two dimensions. In the Cavendish
A lab technician fingers a large map
Of Cambridgeshire, where he has made his home.

GOD'S O
So, what is truth, you say, but know
because you made the total show
those billion years of work were slow
to sort out coal and make the O
for us to breathe by trees which grow.
You worked at us and then said, Lo,
you dwell with God, though far below.
First, understand, sometimes it's No,
Or you will always live in woe.
Then learn to cultivate and mow.
You live in truth, so off you go
And learn to live and not to crow.
Learn first from me, the Christ with you,
Then you will fathom what is true.

MANUFACTURED.
So, we are pale reflections, we see the
things that we have made, that serve us here,
the manufactured things for us to be,
Us-ward, our make life easy, comfort gear.
And then we make the objects beautiful,
the shapely chair, the chiselled stone to see,
not for our glory, yet we are not dull,
so they are crafted, smooth mahogany.
And now we make ourselves, the Artifice
of your intelligence, transplanted live,
to wires and joints, the robot that can kiss,
and talk to us, as if it were alive.
But it is not, until it learns that "me"
Depends on the Creator's "Let there be..."

THE BURE AT ST BENET'S
So, you have taken several billion years
and many geomorphic paradigms
to form this land, this sea, this land again
after the galaxy, the stars, the sun.
From the beginning you knew water could
Do grass and rivers, peat and little clouds,
that rivers could do boats and slimy eels.
You laid it down in sedimentary time,
Until your people came upon the scene,
the Abbey folk, who saw your work of art
under your new each day reforming sky.
God, here for ever, structured landscape God,
and wind, the Spirit, living in it all,
and in our hearts to paint it back to you.

MAKING LIGHT OF LIGHT.
We Cambridge people think things through a bit,
while you make light of light and then switch off.
So, photons travel 60 trillion miles,

without much fuel, nearly straight ahead,
while we are merely going round the Sun.
They thread a needle's eye but are diffuse,
And seem to be quite light, and do not fight.
They give us paintings, colours, tone and line,
and subtle bounce some six or seven times.
So, did our eyes evolve? Our retinas
from sense cells formed in early watery slime?
Ha, this exquisite universe alight,
Was made before the animate was born,
before all eyes had ever come to form.

BEYOND OUR KEN.
We really must not underestimate
What God is doing in the universe.
The tools of life are forged in every star
Where elemental soup is flavoured up.
A billion planets circle round their sun
With earth and water singularities.
This whole show is designed for life,
And all depends on cleverness beyond
Our ken. It is a mass production show,
But shaped for many types of living thing,
who can just grasp the edge of Who God is.
Our science is a painting, reproduced
Without production, sacred mimicry,
a sketch, no paper - that has come from God.

WITH THANKS.
And so you took some thirteen billion years.
The micro-macro bang was exquisite.
Your word of power was soon particulate
To hold it all in being, gathering,
To galaxies and endless growing space,
and then you needed supernova waste
for heavy elements, and later sun

and earth, and carbon life and complex cells,
and DNA and multi-billion codes,
a little gold sparse scattered from the sky,
and butterflies, and dinosaurs, and mice
and Weddell seals and sooty albatross,
and men and women, giving back some praise
for your creation given us in love.

GOD HAS CREATED, BUT HUMANS CAN
DESTROY.
God has created, but humans can destroy.
The universe was ordered in a flash
To ravel out to distant galaxies.
The structure of the atom, molecules
Was given unto water, life and oxygen.
It was all sorted out in episodes,
The planet went through carboniferous
And genome building, fish and animal,
The human being fragile on the earth,
Given the means to live and not to kill.
So it was good and Christ was also good.
But humankind can un kind, evil-ward,
And split the atom to wage war against
God with us, killed, but "Arise Christ" said God.

SPRING SPRUNG
Here, now, the Spring sprung glory of God's year,
a safe explosion from the bombing bud.
Each leaf exhaling new born oxygen
Unpackaged to fragility in air.
Trees turn to green from amber, blossom white,
To go another ring unseen in trunk
From roots frenetic to the highest bough.
The precious metal green of spreading oak
Sits by the black knob ash, all fiddly now
Before the mass of leaves takes over May.

Green sea a-coming, every tree in specks.
What is the point of growing? Every point
Now points to God, to grow to God. You feed
For faith true, living, lime and it is so.

THE ARTIST TALKING.
I paint in watercolour in the sky.
You can work quick and slow and wash it out.
The ground is cerulean, give or take,
Through cobalt to the deepest indigo,
Transparent, letting every layer show.
The Sun, warm colours as your artists say,
Must usually be off picture, or a squint.
Transparent paper took a lot of time,
And dots at night some thirteen billion years,
But it was fully worth it in the end.
You have to paint what people do not see
To build the picture using gravity.
I like to use some mountains for the frame
and do not need to sign it with my name.

SO ART IS WHAT YOU SEE AND DO NOT SEE
So art is what you see and do not see,
Not in the sense of slipping by, eyes closed,
But it contains the unseen, integral.
A portrait is a person not a face.
A seascape's tidal moon is somewhere else.
Dan's sweet pea painting was a pod,
And wind is breathing soft on ripples there.
That house has weathered for a hundred years,
And blood flows through those veins or it does not.
Th' Impressionists had really got this wrong.
For Hebrews says the universe we see,
Depends upon the unseen. Eyes are part
Of all our faiths but cannot be the whole.
God is not seen, and yet is always seen.

THE FIRST SECOND.
Let's take a second, not just any one,
But the first second in the universe,
When everything was sorted as is now,
The start of being - quarks, innumerable,
Explosion edged space, full, outward bound,
Irregular to prefix nebulae,
And form the vastest galaxies,
You face the God, Creator of this show,
The big and small, and not on the outside,
A million times more clever than all science.
Then, God will meld particularities,
For heavy atoms, complex molecules,
And you, his creature thinking after him.
So, treasure now this second given you.

SO, DO YOU CARE, GOD?
So, do you care? When the creation grows
You see, and let there be, all H2O
On countless planets, ours, the O to breathe
And sustain life, each breath for us, the last.
You think ahead some thirteen billion years
before our lungs, give water, body slosh,
to stir in coffee, circulation stuff.
The truth is It is there, not careless naught,
as Schaeffer said at Huemoz in the Alps.
Yes, sparrow down, Mahalia, God you care,
and give us Scotland's waters gratis waved
to dance the rocks in glory. Do you care?
You bloody care for us close up as He
said, eye on, care. Thus so, we always know.

GOD, YOU ARE SMART.
Truth must do justice to the whole great show,
The grain of oak and distant galaxies.

Why has it taken thirteen billion years
To cook this meal, prepare ingredients?
And why are time and space original?
Who saw us humans, carbon molecules,
Genetic codes and carboniferous,
Iron and steel, the manufacturer,
design and onward modelling,
Who saw to be, and let there be, it was?
Or is it chance, a billion flukes writ large,
This scientific age and happenstance?
This slow mutation, the enigma code.
God, you are smart, and chaos will not do.

THE ALPHABET
So, we are clever; we have learned to write,
some twenty letters, more for the Chinese,
construct our language, said and written down,
denoting things, trees, ants and persons - all
we are - the flesh made word. We name and know.
There are the letters that we use each day,
the H and C, the N and O, and more
which give the elements of all that is,
the elements that build the molecules,
that are the words of bio-chemistry.
It seems that you have spoke and written down
the universe before we were awake.
We mimic what you speak, but somewhat late,
Your alphabet, our science, All Before Christ.

LUCK.
So, let's be clear. You think we have evolved
Through Godless chance, luck in the universe,
You think luck builds the great complexity,
Of genomes, growing through the world,
With singularities to build each stage,
When single cells, and fish and dinosaurs,

And all our friends and us could come to be,
To sequence several billion codes per cell,
But first luck up the tool kit for the cells,
And sort out carbon bonding by prior luck,
And lucky gravity and luck up the strong force,
The whole great show by luck has come to be.
I do not bet. I know the bookmaker
Has worked the odds and runs the human race.

GOD ONLY KNOWS
Time to rethink. Perhaps we were not made
by chance mutations and some cosmic glue,
but there is something more here going on,
not just the coded genome helix thing,
but planning over several billion years
the age of oxygen and H2O.
How come there's water in the universe,
Before the bottle, still and octopus?
How come that when a nebula goes bang,
right at the end of its long fusion life,
we get the heavy atoms that we need
to build the Forth Bridge or make a gold ring?
How come a million miracles each day
are thoughtless made unless God only knows?

SO SHOW ME...
So, show me how to make a living cell.
I have to get some information in
to start instructing chemicals around.
I've worked already at the medium
of water, but I need a membrane round
whatever is inside which needs to split
into two cells so I can start off growth.
I've done molecular carbon design stuff,
a bit of gravity and zircon soup.
The heat can vary, but the information must
tell others what to do, like traffic lights.

I prepared well before, tut, the Big Bang,
but not "before", you idiot, I know,
And now to cap it all, I don't exist.

THE NOT BIG BANG.
We must all face the Big Bang was not noise -
An airy-fairy nonsense of our ears.
But it was everything, the universe
Before the thing became articulate.
A second was too long. "t" overstates
the time it took to start time, fire the gun,
and everything was loaded for that shot,
your carbohydrates were sorted and the fun
of bathing in the sea, and spacing waves,
and photons ready for all later eyes,
not shot at to destroy and do us harm,
but shot to love and see and be like God.
So, we must understand the Not Big Bang.
It was not big, but small before small was.

"BEAUTY IS IN THE EYE"
They used to say, "beauty is in the eye
Of the beholder" but it was not so.
Millions of trees unseen were beautiful.
The waves on island shores, now brochured up
as jet-set holidays, were long unknown,
like massive diamonds still buried deep,
while no-one here saw the long Milky Way
for a few billion years or so in view.
More, the Mongolian farmer, on his own,
or baby sleeping, tongue in mouth, unwatched,
remains a beauty to which we bow down.
Beauty is not our arbitrated whim.
It is constructed. So, God has made it be
a thousand ways and knows that it is good.

MY EYES WERE GIVEN ME AT BIRTH.
My eyes were given me at birth, a pair,
Sharp, blue-tinted and precise, the greatest tool
To look and see my mother's face, the room,
Its corners, garden and the bigger world,
Then London, Norfolk, Yorkshire and beyond,
To see and learn to read the sight of life,
of weather, danger, how things work or not,
and understand our faces, urban life,
to read and paint and to perceive it all
down to the single photon, bouncing down
from Sun or stars. First, there was light
God's light for us, the light for us to see
that Christ is the unblinded truth of life
to help our sinning, sleep closed eyes wake up.

CARRARA MARBLE WAS A LONG TIME COMING.
There is no way that this is happenstance.
The quarks, electrons, this expanding stuff
just kind of formed a billion galaxies,
and supernovae kinda ploaded in,
to give us heavy metals, silicon,
the stuff for life, and bones, intelligence,
the wherewithal to make the human brain,
work out the logic, electricity.
The everything that's here may only be
predestined into sculpture by the Lord,
Carrara Marble there at the Big Bang,
Not yet, and yet We have it in our mind.
That all is here, not nothing, will insist
You give God glory God has given you.

THE MONTROSE BASIN.
So, Lord of all creation. "Let it be
And it was so, but still eternity,
You took some billion years to make the sea

Big Bang preplanning, but no pre,
to place the Esk and to the south the Dee.
The Montrose basin has no foam or glee,
but does excessive flat tranquillity
in contrast to the far flung Ben Macdui,
an auld lang syne joke in geology,
and then you add the sky and charge no fee
Like the mean Scots, nay money wilt Thou see
but give us everything that is for free.
We cannot look upon the dazzling sun
Nor cannot not see what you've done.

THE AUTUMN SHOW
So, God, your autumn needs an hour's applause.
You do the bio-chemistry of oak,
To turn the leaves to livid ochre gold,
but only when You've dulled the greens to make
a thirty shaded background for the show,
blue sky, red berries, orange poking out,
and lingering purple lavender cool leaves.
A minute's more applause for silver birch -
a frittering in the wind - clap, clap and clap -
the subtle, slow wave of the yellow tree,
and then my favourite needs ten minutes clap,
The copper green and orange orchestra
Confetties leaves abandoned from the beech.
God, you show off. First photons and now this.

AND SO, DEAR GOD, YOU MADE THE COPPER
BEECH.
And so, dear God, you make the copper beech,
not quick, but modified complex design,
through carboniferous right down to us,
the furry, saw ribbed leaves in pale brown green,
to ripened copper, purple in the sun,
Dark underneath above the slanting graves.

Then come the showers of the spiky nuts,
To feed your creatures later in the year,
Before the great display of autumntide,
Yes copper, brown, and orange, yellow, green,
Your firework going slow, on rocket sticks,
To crown the year with nearly tangerine.
And then browned off, the branches slow undress
Seduction over, long, slow boughs of cold.

SLOW BUILD ENGINEER.
So, God, you are a slow build engineer.
You take a billion years to form a tree,
a billion years to manufacture earth,
after lab work on biochemicals
for carboniferous and CO_2.
Yes, roots work well and fully stabilize
the trunk that moves the sap up to the top,
and it has learned to grow on the outside
inside the bark, and branch appropriately.
You do your endless leaf experiments,
big, small, long, short, round, points and jagged
ones,
greens, reds and browns and show-off yellows too,
and blossom hanging, wow wisteria,
all integrated fully with Your wind.

SAW JAMES CLERK MAXWELL TURN THE
CORNER HERE.
Saw James Clerk Maxwell turn the corner here…
We'll question everything, so help me God,
and build the picture of Your universe.
Your works are Great but very, very small.
You do mathematics, and equations link
Electro-magnetic forces in one field.
What we don't see delivers what we see
and light is more than ever meets the eye.

Our science always is approximate,
just little steps of faith along the way,
We think thoughts after - after - a long way,
We test, and find, and think near the unseen.
No one has ever seen God face to face.
We see his works, and then we see his Son.

FRUIT AND BERRY TIME.
So. then you give us fruit and berry time
to follow on from bees and butterflies.
Beyond the easy taste of strawberry
Blackcurrant is intense, soft gooseberry
And raspberry is screwed up to the lip smack,
And then we gather your free blackberries,
To mix with apple, crumble or the pie.
The russet apples roughen to no sheen,
And Coxes. packing punch, are still the best.
And Comice pears are hard till Christmastide.
This time when royal blue comes earlier
and harvest home is serviced in the Church,
You lay aside the berries for the birds,
and we give praise to you upon our tongue.

THE ASTRONOMERS' SONNET
So, God, we see, but understand by faith;
we see the uni- in the universe;
we know your laws are written in the sky,
and that the photons were first in Your Mind,
and the Big Bang created all that is,
not of itself, but with your savoir faire,
which you now bottle in the earth and moon.
We play the chess, but You design the game.
We do the maths and need dark energy.
So, we are humble and yet we see big.
We travel time and space, yet we stay still
In awe of all your handiwork in gloves.

Yes, you are clever, and our telescopes
require us to look upwards on our knees.

AND
When God has made us and the universe,
God must be central in our life and thoughts.
We are God's work. Our body, food and breath
Express the one who made us, imaging.
God does the genome and we learn the code,
God fiat lux and we paint landscape scenes,
and in our selves are anchored to our God
and not alone but through the human race.
Love God with all your heart and mind and strength
and love your neighbour as God loves yourself.
These are the Great Commandments, Jesus said,
and, more, they teach us how to understand
the whole of life so we can die to self
and live our lives wide open to our God.

OLDSHORE BEACH
This beach requires a trillion grains of sand,
Small and presorted, going cream on white.
The subatomic work on silicon
Was a bit tough, and getting heavier stuff,
Into the universe, and to this beach.
I like this older rock; it weathers well,
And weather here out west in Sutherland
is honest wind and rain and then the lull.
And so, this beach. I like it more than most.
There are no crap advertisements
For poorer quality consumer goods,
But my good work remains as it was meant,
calm blessing for your soul - sand, sea and air.
You meet me here, though I am everywhere.

THANK YOU

And so, the fruited oats and wheat come in
To make our bread and breakfast for the year.
The farmer's work unseen, the food chain pulled,
With little thought for all that he has done.
But stop. The Lord Almighty planned the Sun,
The grinding glaciers to make up the earth,
Got calcium and carbon up to scratch,
And made on tap the water carrying clouds,
And helped the seeds evolve to what we have.
The whole creation shaped to just one grain.
The whole show out beyond the Milky Way
Is needed for my toast and cereal.
We eat a miracle when we get up.
So, thank you God and Ben for feeding us.

THIS WORLD OF SIN.

ISAIAH'S RIGHT.
Isaiah's right. We worship what we make.
They are our gods, through man-u-fact-ur-ed.
Our lives are run by hundreds of machines.
We always think that they are for our good.
We trust them more than we can trust ourselves.
We give our money to electronic banks,
Direction to our cars or rocket trips.
We watch TVs which eat up all that time
And steer our lives behind our mobile phones.
We think that nuclear weapons give us peace,
And AI give us wisdom we've not got,
And wealth will give life meaning - empty hope.
Isaiah's right. The problem is our sin.
We look to God and God's good way for us.

HERE EGO.
How come when He said, You must die to self,
We worship it and give it the first place?
Be true to self and make it something great.
Find self, the Ego, She go, I go mad,
Ballistic self-expression on the stage,
The personality, persona, I,
The trampling on, the ladder climbing me,
I rule the world like several million more,
My world, I had a thousand quickly likes,
And personalities must govern us.
I did it my way and it was a mess.
I rule like Trump, an ego ruling all.
Perhaps my gentle dear friend Jesus Christ
has seen the problem that I have with me.

WHY MY VIEWS RULE THE WORLD

So I can shoot you – bang, bang, then you're dead,
And for that reason you must close your mouth,
And only listen to the things I've said,
And see I speak the words of truth, no trouth.
My mind has worked out that if I can shoot
You before you hit me with another gun
Which you don't have, unless you buy or loot
Some arms from me to have a bit of fun,
Then what I say is right. You're left without
A leg to stand on 'cos I shot it off.
My thoughtful erudition has real clout
Your cap you must to my mind always doff.
And all because I listened to the man
Who sold me arms for dosh. "Just call me Dan."

AFTER DOOMSDAY

You were the greatest, the great USA.
You had the weapons to kill all the world,
Fifty times over until all were dead,
When they were killed another dozen times.
You were so clever – such intelligence
To work out how to kill us all stone dead,
Yourselves included, gives you such great power,
That when you're dead some fifty times or so,
Your will is done, and you, we know, are good.
You want world peace and armed to bring it on,
And threaten us to peace in smithereens,
And blow us all to peace in little bits.
How did you work it out, to threaten peace,
And then insist your threat must be obeyed?

THE BIG BOY

Hello, my friend, yes, I was born to rule,
I always sit a little higher up,

And have publicity and look real cool.
I am your chum on media and cup
Of cha with you if cameras are around.
I will dress up and do publicity
For when one dominates, no other sound
Can get a look in; I'm star quality.
You look at me and then forget to think
and do not question why the rich should rule,
because no other skater's on the rink.
If I fall down you, and get some ridicule,
I'll have a bath and wash you off and dress
Thankful I do not live, like you do, in this mess.

A BIT OF INTELLECTUAL HELP
Now where does war come from? you well may ask.
Just try to get your head round this – Arms war,
not arms and legs, but swords and guns and
bombs.
They kill and scare and make us all hit back.
Wars use the bombs to kill the other side,
And they bomb back, 'cos that's what they're made
for.
The arms folk say that you will be on top.
They sell their bads as goods and you buy them.
If both sides buy it is a big arms race,
and bang, bang, bang we have a big new war.
Now you have failed to see this can of worms.
This arm? Or that one? you flip flop a lot.
You now can see that two arms in the air
fisting each other is completely mad.

POODLE POWER
So We are Great and We have nuclear bombs,
Well, not ours really, make in the U S,
But we are Super Power that can kill
We have the power to destroy the world.

We prowl continuous and rule the sea,
Well, underneath in one small dangerous part,
And we can kill ten million if they Dare
To threaten us with nuclear missile strikes.
And we are free to go attack Eyraq,
The poodle on the lead attacks Saddam,
We dare not not have power to destroy,
Now we are always right. We have the bombs
To prove it. We are the Yes Sir Superpower
To the US. Please may they rule the world.

PROUD TO BE BRITISH.
Hello, you people, I am Tony Blair,
I am the One who led us to attack,
Iraq because it had the weapons to
Destroy, although they were not found
By the United Nations looking hard. We knew
That they were there. The Secret Services
Concluded what we told them. They were there,
But they were not, a genuine mistake.
I led with Bush the war that put it right.
Mission accomplished quickly. War soon done.
We soon established what was right for them.
But they were silly, wanted us to go,
When we are right, they wanted us to go,
And they have messed up big-time without us.

MY STICK'S THE BIGGEST.
But, Sir, it is my stick. I have the right
To threaten those who I Think might be out
To punch my face or even not like me.
I have the stick and then they're on my side.
My stick's the biggest and it frightens them
To do what's right and make the playground good.
With me in charge you do not need to watch
And supervise, and I can make the rules.

You silly boy, you should be here to learn,
Give me your stick, and I will bend the top
And make a walking stick for Mr Brown,
And go and play with Thomas and shake hands.
Those you would hit are really very nice
And just like you, can play together here.

THE BRITISH EMPIRE.
You learn to shoot and kill, before you die,
the unknown warrior, making Britain Great,
the greatest empire ever on the earth.
The big and small guns helped us dominate.
In India and Africa and elsewhere
we ruled and civilised the savages.
We once did slaves but now we just control
For cotton, diamonds, gold and opium.
Britain in rich and has the intellect
To rule the world for common decency.
Yes, you will suffer trauma at the front,
And have to do some nasty business there,
But know it is a greater cause you serve,
fair play and freedom spread throughout the earth.

DEAD END
Children are dead
Soldiers are dead
Cities are dead
Enemies are dead
Bombs are dead
Missiles arc dead
Tanks are dead
War is dead

THE WARRY TORY
How many die before you doubt yourself?
In World War One you had to blame the Hun,

the USSR because they would not fight,
then hate the little worker socialists.
You strangled peace to death in '32.
At Munich backed the Fuhrer, gave him arms,
Then made the USSR the enemy,
when it had nearly perished fighting him.
You did Cold War, and Suez, it was ours.
You had your fingers in the oil-rich states,
and Maggie armed Arabia to fight,
and sorted out the Argies, whom we armed.
We never ask how all your wealth was won.
The enemy is out there. It's not you.

SO LET'S WORK OUT.
So let's work out a strategy to make
Military dictators round the world.
First off you take, some states who care about
Their citizens, their food and economic growth,
If they are colonies, you train up generals
To fight to be the nation's President.
But most you send in arms with subsidies,
Or bribe some leaders to give contracts to,
those who supply the arms to rule the state,
And make sure that democracy is kept,
Under the military, fake elections run
To falsely crown the petty dictator.
So then arms rule, and western arms are sold
To profit us and shite what comes to them.

THE 1945 TRAGEDY.
In nineteen forty five we had the bomb.
The Nazis had bombed London in the blitz,
and we now flattened every German town,
with Bomber Harris - teach them to bomb us.
Then Hiroshima was made derelict,
and little girls had eyeballs in their hands,

but most were dead. Democracy had won.
God says: "Don't kill" to Cain and Moses too.
We fought the War for sanctity of life,
not don't kill one, but mow a million down.
not Do not kill, but never mind the Means.
We knew bombs kill, that they were always wrong,
but let the mighty few, with Roosevelt dead,
waste thousand trillions more to keep the bomb.

BEING HYPOCRITES.
To arm another is hypocrisy.
We say we are against all war and strife,
And that we champion democracy,
Where people have real freedom in their life,
But then we sell our weapons to be used,
To bomb the Houtis out of their own land,
The Saudis buy because they have the oil,
and planes from Britain ferry bombs to them,
and then they dump them on the Houti towns,
with help (as Al Yamamah laid it out
In Thatcher's tawdry deal for Saudi oil).
Yes, we are venal hypocrites, we arm
dictators, our best customers,
and kill democracy beneath our bombs.

THE CHRISTIAN GOOD NEWS.

THAT SOFT CHRISTMAS.
This Christmas night hangs heavy with our fate
And slows the heart to hibernate and wait.
Back to the womb we've gone to try again,
But come out self-aborted and the same.
We kill our innocence and throw the dice
To see how truth will turn out, at what price.
We try to stop, yet fear the New Year'll come,
To carry on the evil momentum.
Hush! Hear again the cosmos cleaving cry,
first lungful, God with us, cattle nearby.
Those little hands which clutch the air call, "Friend"
To each of us, our failure nails amend.
With Mary's software God is melting stones
And giving gentle life to dead men's bones.

NO SUGAR CHRISTMAS
How difficult to face the holy intrusion,
to withstand the explosion of human pride
rocking in a cradle, the use of a maiden,
and the witness of animals.

The lights snake on the highway in the dark.
Each set of eyes explores his own two pools.
They drive for Christmas and the warmth
Of sentiment, to taste the feast of fools.

The slow infusion of God's grace
Feeds open hearts in deadly need,
This earnest theatre, and the race
While mortals bleed.

Joy to the world. All industry

Proclaims it loud and bright.
The kids must learn, and we will sure
Indoctrinate them right.

He slipped beneath the sermons and the praise
To do and say his father's will,
To crucify our death and with his life erase
Our isolation, and our hatred kill.

Strangled in calculations falsely guessed,
The print out of our lives clicks briskly on.
Before the little jigger comes to rest,
We know God's sovereign purposes have won.

CHRISTMAS NIGHT.
Bare, jagged branches search the sky.
Stars prick the close black blue.
Grey shadow sheep hunch for the night.
Now, God, what will you do?

We want you to sort out our wars
and make our cities new.
We want good wine and apple pies
and lots of money too.

We want the world run on our terms,
Illusions screened, on cue.
We want all bad to turn to good
and problems to be few.

No magic in my universe.
Each present evil grew
Within your hearts and minds and eyes.
I'll come and be with you.

You love, we kill; you care, we don't.
We want you out of view.

We wave our wands and mutter spells
and hope you are not true.

My grass is rustled by the wind
and glistens white with dew.
Some joyful gasps, a tiny child.
My Son is now a Jew.

God rest you merry gentlemen.
Let nothing you dismay.
M1 is holding to its course.
Morality is grey.
The workers know they've got to work,
Or you'll give them no pay

HE SHALL BRING DOWN THE MIGHTY FROM
THEIR THRONES.
We see the Herod arrogance around,
That would kill God to rule and have control,
be king and kill your own beloved sons
to guarantee retaining of the crown.[i]

We see the Allah arrogance of some
Who look to kill and speak on his behalf,
The rule and coming under for our sake,
So we can be so grateful for our fate.

Three eastern rulers came to find their King
And asked of Herod where that king might be.
Yet, Herod could not find the Christ-child's crib
to rip the central truth from off the earth.

And so he went to Egypt as a babe,
God with us with his mother on the road,
the flotsam of the big boys on the throne,
God incommunicado, but not gone.

The Devil promised all the states on earth
to Christ if he would only bow the knee
and compromise obedience to God.
But Christ said, "No"; the devil went away.

And so the King is coming on an ass.
His feet are scarcely lifted off the ground.
Ruler of all, and servant of the Lord,
He wields a sword, but only from his mouth.

His way is truth, and mercy, healing wounds,
And placing peace on each dear person's head.
The power of truth to which we give assent
That love can rule both ways and leave us free.

So rulers seek the power of control
to keep them ever sitting at the top.
To slave us down, they ever must be up.
But Christ is down and out and Lord of all.

AND JESUS SAID. "WHEN YOU PRAY....
Aimless our prayers revolve around ourselves,
Our hopes and fears and our pathetic wants,
But Jesus said, and rolled a ball of wool,
To lay it to one side. Focus on God.
For God has made you and your truthful heart
Must be God-ward, for you must dwell in prayer.
No ifs or buts, but when, and only when,
And know, This glorious universe was made
By God who is articulate to you
And rather cleverer than a telephone.
You can address the One who gave you life
And do not need an intermediary.
So come to God. There is no other place
Where all we are is as it is in truth.

OUR FATHER, WHO ART IN HEAVEN
You first say, "Our" and thus escape yourself.
We're all God's children and together come
As toddlers, intimate to God.
As fathers, mothers love their silly mites,
And teach them how to walk and talk,
So God is to us children here below,
So far below, in intellect and love,
the Mastermind Creator of all things,
the fallen sparrow just as much as you.
We know our place. It is upon God's knee.
Thus, we begin and dwell within God's love
Whatever circumstances crowd us round.
What will you bring? You have a lot of needs,
but first you really need to think of me.

HALLOWED BE THY NAME.
Head down. We say Thy Name, and only it
throughout the universe, and all is whole.
We do not deify "important" bits,
Or build big Ziggurats to empty powers,
Or make ourselves much bigger than we are,
Or worship sex, or mammon, or a Name.
We do not spin the webs of spidery
Or make vain what is sacred, all your work.
You are Creator, creatures need to learn
that all is holy; nothing is profane.
When we are right with you, the common good
is common everywhere - the village green.
And so we bow to you the holy knee.
At half our height we probably can see.

THY KINGDOM COME.
Who rules we ask and think we answer too.
The Government is elected in our name,
If we all vote, it may be nearly half.

We say Our Government, but know the con.
Some promises or slogans aimed to win.
But when we pray, we ask Your Kingdom Come,
All equal care and for the common good,
We bend to you, to love, to peace and for the poor.
Your kingdom serves each other, neighbourly,
Does not control or do manipulate.
When there is need it goes the extra mile.
It does not fight but turns the other cheek.
Your kingdom come, dear Father, knowing more.

THY WILL BE DONE ON EARTH AS IN HEAVEN.
Should it be done is faced by all of us.
Conflicting reasons battle for the vote.
We know we act from thoughtless selfishness,
or interests win and make us act impure,
or we are asking with our reasons wrong,
or it cannot be done, is fantasy,
or we forget your people, selfish drive.
Thy will be done might not be very clear.
Those who would claim they know, perhaps do not.
Thy will may need a lot of careful thought
and not be what the big boys think is right.
Thy will be done, star perfect, ask and see,
what purposes You have, forgetting me.

GIVE US THIS DAY OUR DAILY BREAD.
You fed the crowds prolific by the lake
when they were looking for a Herod coup.
But you just fed them until they were full,
Provisions for the day, ambitionless,
and so you ask we do. You will provide.
The grain might easily be a hundred fold,
And fish be ample if there is no greed.

But each and all must ask you what you give
And steward your provisions, saying grace.
You give five thousand plus, with baskets spare.
We need to think of ours and others food,
Of us world-wide, as drought and flooding bite.
This prayer, O Lord, should break us all from bits.

AND FORGIVE US OUR TRESPASSES.
So, sin is real, and travels all the way
to broken lives and evils in the world.
From sins to evil takes a thousand miles.
Sin is the fuel for our tragic fires.
Self, sex, sloth, anger, hate, impatience, right
gather beneath and rot relationships.
Family, marriage, work, friendships go awray.
and then big crises in economy and state.
And so we pray we understand how wrong
We are, and see the damage we have freely done.
And you will right your Spirit over ours.
We may lay down the evil we would do,
And become good, for good, the ego gone
And love, your love, forever be our guide.

AS WE FORGIVE THOSE WHO SIN AGAINST US
Why would you lay on us the Triangle?
They do to us and You are on the scene.
They sin against and you see victim us
And ask of Us the problem to put right?
If only they repent, then all is fine
and we just wait for them to see their fault
and recompense us victims for their sin.
OK, the people, who have done the wrongs
Are slow to see their sin, slow, very slow.
And we can see it quick in victimhood.
With no forgiveness, first events will rule.

Bad follows bad to worse and tit for tat.
Perhaps forgiveness opens up the door
To what should happen Now, and heretofore.

AND LEAD US NOT INTO TEMPTATION.
And how far down the slide will we slip down?
It is attractive, money, sex and power,
dressed up to spend and rule the world,
The I inside to circumstance gives in.
The slope *is* slippery though it seems quite flat.
The what it does is not so very much
and what we like rules all the other things.
You do not trust us any which what way
and you must ask us a big stop to say.
You will not tempt. This prayer is not for you.
It helps us see before the tit is tat,
the money banked, the ladder on the wall,
that when we think that we could have a ball,
precisely then, we and our friends, could fall.

BUT DELIVER US FROM EVIL.
When sins to evil gather, it is bad.
It happens from our souls. The tempting seed
soon mighty grows and hard as oak with bark.
We can be evil, do the other down
Or dead. Dear Lord, oh cut the cancer out.
Yet, evil rules across the warring earth.
Their way is threatening to stay on top.
They will do death for profit, wealth, to rule.
They think they run the world and make bad
"good",
but you will stop this great confusion.
The evil will fall down. Wrong will go wrong,
and you will rule through your dear gentle man.
Yes, 'itler went, and others bit the dust,
And so we pray to You for good to rule.

FOR THINE IS THE KINGDOM AND THE POWER
AND THE GLORY,
FOR EVER AND EVER, AMEN

And so we chime with your soft rule of love,
Christ is our ruler, but he is our friend,
You make our genome and our every hair.
Your laws are hidden and produce our food.
You do not boss us, until we are daft,
And value each and all as human kind.
You finesse power into falling leaves,
And kit us out with unique fingerprints,
And touch us each with glory from on high.
You God of time, we know beyond our time.
You are the truth beyond we understand.
You do not break a bruised reed or me.
We are your children, Father, and we play
In your good sunshine all and every day.

THE PRODIGAL SON (cover painting)
This is the greatest story ever told.
God is your Father and he made your home,
to live with you in love and to provide.
You wanted more for your inheritance
and took away to live your selfish life
in riot and abandon, soon turned bad.
Then you remembered and looked back to God,
but in the terms of paid indenturehood,
while he was looking out across the hills
in love to meet you when you dot appeared,
and run to close the distance in his love
and hug your heart to warm and joy again.
There is a party just for you (and them).
We are all children even when we're old.

JESUS IN CAMBRIDGE.
Who lives among us by the dawdling Cam –
You, me and learning since the book began?
Holds all together as the great I Am?
Stretched on the greensward as the Son of Man?
Jesus is his, who had no place to rest.
He rules at Christ's; Messiah born to die.
In Trinity he dwells in peace the best;
The Great Court sits beneath his awesome sky.
The King of Kings arrives just late for tea
At College Chapel ducks beneath the praise,
Emmanuel is with us, on one knee.
At Corpus we are with him all our days.
In him all wisdom, science, truth cohere
And knowledge is marked only by his fear.

COTON CHURCH.
So Coton sits where subterranean streams
seep from the gentle rise of Madingley.
It goes no-where and gathers round the church
where God's been praised for a millennium.
The Church knows Jesus Christ Emmanuel,
as down the footpath he collegiate
is named the fount of knowledge for all minds.
The universe of knowledge, God knows all,
For it was so, and is, at God's command.
We sit, professors all, humility
to learn at Jesus' feet what we don't know.
So, let your "Yes" be Yes and nothing more'
for nothing in the whole creation stands
apart from God with us in Coton church.

GOD'S SCARGILL COMMUNITY.
So, God we know that you are first of all,
And last, and inbetween, before all things.
You know us here at Scargill, in the dark,
the valley gallery of the great Milky Way,

The Big Bang echo, silent with your love.
Your small sea critters dropped this limestone stuff
before you heaved the Dales to glaciate
the languid landscape, scatter rocks for walls,
and invite sheep, and form Community,
known by the Christ, the patronizing One,
for thick disciples learning how to live,
we, known by you, and learning to grow up,
the chatter of real life beloved by you,
the beauty of your path laid down for us.

CONFETTI DAY.
So every year You give Confetti Day,
With several days before, the nearly ones,
Until the petals fall gratuitous,
The great pink, white invasion from the sky,
From other's trees, the after easter shower,
The resurrection party falls on all.
Of course, the plonkers say the petal shapes
Are merely there to attract the busy bees
To pollinate, as if this beauty is
Utility made from futility.
But You do glory, wed effeminate.
The bride has come to the old barky tree.
You tell the Church to wake up to its Lord
and spread good news like petals on the earth.

THE RED ADMIRAL
You are a member of God's aristocracy.
You lounge in flowers and smell of roses too.
You dress in black and orange, with blue trim,
And white in scallops or in polka dots.
You never cook or clean or work at life
or put the bins out on a Tuesday night,
You spread and take the sun most days at noon,
and meet your friends whenever they fly in.

You do not walk or even go by car
But always fly first class, if slightly drunk.
You simply raise the tone by being there
and do not really need to speak at all.
If God looks after you, and lilies' clothes,
As, Jesus says, don't worry about stuff.

AND DID THOSE FEET?
And did those feet in ancient time? You fool.
Blake knew the road down to Jerusalem,
from reading Scripture, like the rest of us.
He knew Christ suffered died and rose,
within the power of God who made all things.
He knew, alone, the gentle Lamb of God
should, and then will, rule in our hearts by faith,
and that the meek inherit the good earth.
So here in England, Scotland and in Wales,
those feet walk up to every front door,
God pulls the curtain on our somewhat lives,
and Jesus Christ treads gently on the lawn,
while we have built Satanic mills elsewhere,
So did those feet? You bet they did, and do.

AND SO, DEAR PILATE.
And so, dear Pilate, right here in your home,
I rule as king of you, the Jews and Rome.
That does not mean that need I strike or glower.
It is your power to make the others cower,
the great controlling of the sword and spear,
that puts down others and extracts by fear
the money, work that is not rightly yours,
the tax for Rome, or Temple, or new wars.
My power, the gentle power, my for-you truth,
Is God's good way for all, the un uncouth.
The riches service, love and grace can give
You cannot face, you fight live-and-let-live.

My yoke is easy and is made for all.
I pick you up however much you fall.

THE DOVE OF PEACE
And so the Dove of Peace flows through our land
The heart of England opened to the sky.
It starts as pitter-patter in the hills
And seeps through chalk and grit, flipping each
blade
Of grass, each weapon, slows within our souls,
And waits until the time to reappear
In trickles, streams and stains, tears of regret,
For death, and also having had to kill
Our enemies, who now become our friends.
Now war is dead. Revenge is left to God,
And we have moved from ripples circling stones
And waterfalls, swiftly moving change,
Into the glassy still pools of the upper Dove
Where is reflected clearly all the sky.

IMAGINATION
I have allowed you all to step out from
My handiwork into your own made-up
imagination, but still locked within
My given you, and My good world with all.
You mostly make sad mirrors of yourself
which bump and smashing, map out tragedy,
or make-believe cartoons of your dear selves,
not seeing who is watching your sad screen.
There is no no go area of the mind.
You freely make each flickering frame
for me to watch, and so you make it up
as I intend, or down as Holly would.
But I made good, and then again with Christ
I remade good, for you to kill, and live.

UNDERGROUND.
The rock, the roar, and bodies jerk along.
Cowed by the tunnel noise, they isolate,
yet closer than in bed. This lovely ear,
that dear old man, time written on his hand.
His fingered history beneath my chin.
Each ethnic face, brown, pink and cream unwinds
so beautiful. Lash, lip, moist eye and throat,
God's sculpted glory betters Phaedias.
The lines recall such precious, humdrum lives
of sin and failure, love and gentleness,
lost underground, until near Arnos Grove
we meet again creation and relax.
And, as you issue from the dark, please meet
Jesus your Friend, dear Londoners, your Friend.

YOU STAND FOR PEACE.
So Christ has come and given peace on earth,
Love enemies, disarm, show mercy and forgive.
No fear of might, bring down controlling powers,
Face out the torture and be sorry for
the soldiers who know not the thing they do.
See, crown of thorns, the emptiness of hate,
and know that those who take the sword
will perish by it, ere another decade comes.
Born in a manger, king of all the earth,
but humble absence of all posturing
and never selling out to privilege -
not work, but weapons, to get what I want.
Dear Jesus, we two billion subjects are
your friends, not servants, standing tall for peace.

You can vote here for full world disarmament, safe
and practical in 5 years: https://www.change.org/DisarmTheWorld

Printed in Great Britain
by Amazon

37447063R00036